Original title:
Tropical Tranquility Awaits

Copyright © 2025 Creative Arts Management OÜ
All rights reserved.

Author: Thomas Sinclair
ISBN HARDBACK: 978-1-80581-613-3
ISBN PAPERBACK: 978-1-80581-140-4
ISBN EBOOK: 978-1-80581-613-3

Breaths of Life Amongst the Palms

In a hammock hung up high, oh what a sight,
A pineapple's my pillow, feels just right.
A parrot squawks jokes, it's quite the proud clown,
While coconuts giggle as they fall down.

Sipping on smoothies, my face like a mess,
Mangoes and blueberries, I'm in soft dress.
The sun has a punchline that tickles my toes,
As I trip on my flip-flops and dance with my nose.

The waves play a tune, like a ukulele,
But my sun hat is stealing the show, quite gaily.
I dive in unexpected, make quite the splash,
Even fish stop to laugh as I make my dash.

Palm trees lean in, they are part of the fun,
Whispering secrets of a day in the sun.
With a wink from a crab, the laughter won't cease,
In this goofy oasis, I've found my peace.

Barefoot on the Blissful Beach

Barefoot I run, dodging sandcastles,
The tide rolls in, my shoelaces tangles.
Seagulls squawk, asking for fries,
They dive like they're winning a prize.

The sun's too bright, I squint and laugh,
A crab snickers, it's calculated wrath.
A flip-flop flies, the beach is a stage,
Summer's a clown, turning the page.

Vows of the Soothing Sea

The waves propose, they crash and spray,
I vow to stay, just a little okay.
With salty hugs, they wrap me tight,
I giggle like a kid, what a silly sight.

Fishy friends swim in a ballet,
They dance for me, 'It's your birthday!'
I raise a toast with coconut juice,
The ocean cheers, 'You're my excuse!'

The Emerald Oasis Calls

In a lush retreat where gaggles roam,
I hear the jungle, 'Come back home!'
Chameleons flash, with funky gear,
They wink at me, 'What's your fear?'

Palm trees sway, in a silly jig,
They whisper secrets, 'Dance, don't dig!'
A toucan honks, with a colorful shout,
I laugh so hard, my worries bail out.

Coconuts and Calm Reflections

Coconuts grin, like they know my plight,
They roll around, making me laugh tight.
The breeze tells jokes, it brushes my face,
Each giggle whispers, 'No need for grace!'

Reflections dance on the water's skin,
A silly sea sponge floats with a grin.
I flip my hair, and kick my feet,
In this world of chuckles, life's a treat.

Beyond the Deep-blue Horizon

In a boat made of dreams, we sail,
Chasing fish with a crazy tail.
The ocean laughs, splashes me a wink,
While seagulls plot, it's all in sync.

Sunburned folks dance like they're possessed,
Each wave a jolt, we jest and jest.
The sun dips low, a squishy peach,
Making funny faces, within reach.

Swaying Palms and Silent Thoughts

Palms wave like they're at a show,
A breezy breeze steals my cold soda, though.
Sand casts giggles, it tickles my feet,
While a crab joins in, trying to compete.

Laughter drifts in warm, lazy air,
As flip-flops fly, like they don't care.
A sun hat tips, what a funny sight,
As shadow creatures come out at night.

The Rhythm of a Forgotten Cove

In a cove where time took a nap,
Fishes groove like they're in a trap.
Dancing shells with a jig and twirl,
While sea cucumbers giggle and whirl.

The tide insists it's all a game,
Making me question if I'm to blame.
A whispering wave says, 'Join the fun!',
As my flip-flop flies, watch out, run!

Captured by Sunset's Warm Glow

The sun pulls a curtain, soft and bright,
Painting the sky in a playful fight.
Balloons of clouds puff up and tease,
As sandcastles stand like they're frozen at ease.

The crickets start singing a silly tune,
While cucumbers surf on a silver spoon.
Chuckling at shadows long and spry,
We wave to the sunset, it's time to say bye.

Songs of the Sandy Shore

Sandy toes and sunburned nose,
We dance where the ocean flows.
Seagulls squawk like they own the place,
We giggle, still trying to keep our grace.

Waves crash down, like laughter shared,
In floats we ride, unprepared.
Surfboards flop, we tumble and roll,
Splashing around, it's a comical goal.

Cocktails spill, umbrellas fly,
Sipping our drinks while we wave goodbye.
Sunburnt cheeks, a bright hue of red,
The best kind of fun, that's what we said.

Cradled by the Coastal Calm

Breezes tickle our sun-kissed skin,
We lounge on the beach, let the games begin.
Crabs in shorts race for the prize,
While kids giggle at their funny ties.

Flip-flops lost, where did they go?
Dancing in sand, with much gusto.
Laughter echoes, a joyful sound,
As we chase our hats that fly around.

We sip on drinks, with silly straws,
And giggle at fishes with loud applause.
The sun sets low, painting the scene,
As we make jokes with our sunscreen.

Coconut Groves and Quiet Nights

Coconut hats, a fashion craze,
We sway and laugh in the moonlight's haze.
Palm trees whisper, secrets they keep,
While we snuggle up, drifting to sleep.

Laughter erupts at the monkey's tricks,
He swings like he thinks he's the mix.
Camping under the twinkling sky,
We tell ghost stories that make us cry.

Bugs buzz loudly, a choir they sing,
As we dance around, letting joy take wing.
With marshmallows toasted, laughter ignites,
In this paradise of cozy nights.

Mirage of a Blissful Dream

Waking up to the sun's gentle call,
Dreams of swimming, having a ball.
With snorkels strapped, we're ready to dive,
Bringing laughter to where fish thrive.

We slip and slide on the wet sea floor,
Giggling as we search for treasures galore.
A starfish poses, but we don't care,
Our selfies are silly, with much flair.

The ocean laughs, we laugh too,
With giggles carried by skies so blue.
In this shimmering view, time softly beams,
Where every splash is a part of our dreams.

The Paradise of Peaceful Repose

In hammocks swaying, I take a nap,
My dreams are filled with guava sap.
The seagulls gossip, oh what a sight,
While I debate if it's day or night.

The palm trees chuckle at my slow stroll,
A lizard sunbathes, that's my goal!
Beaches are laughing, the waves play a tune,
As I search for snacks under the moon.

Delicate Dancers of the Night

Fireflies waltz in a twinkling show,
While crickets serenade down below.
I try to dance, but trip on my feet,
The stars just giggle at my defeat.

A coconut falls with a soft plop,
And sends my drink right over the top.
I sip it slow, with a playful pout,
As the night wraps me in a silly clout.

Echoes of Elysian Shores

Seashells whisper tales of the sea,
They talk too much; they won't let me be!
The waves crash in with a comedic roar,
As I chase my hat right back to the shore.

With sand stuck tight to my sunburned nose,
I laugh at the sun as it sets, who knows?
Will it rise again or stay in retreat?
This beach bum's laughter can't be beat.

Flickers of Golden Hour

The sun drips gold on the ocean's face,
Where jellyfish prance in an awkward race.
I join the dance, but step on my toes,
And tip over laughing while the breeze blows.

Snorkels and flippers are spread all around,
But all I can do is float, I have found.
With each silly splash and wave of delight,
This golden hour feels just right.

A Canopy of Comfort

Beneath the leaves, a hammock swings,
With chirping birds that dance and sing.
A coconut drops with a plop, oh dear,
It seems my lunch has made it here!

Sunshine peeks through a leafy screen,
While lizards plot with a sneaky gleam.
Sipping juice that tastes like cheer,
I toast the day; oh, what a year!

A parrot squawks, 'You're looking fine!'
I laugh and sip my drink of lime.
The breeze runs wild, a playful tease,
But all's well in this warm, soft breeze.

As night falls down, and stars come out,
A firefly flickers; there's no doubt.
With alligators in a chatty spree,
This funny life is just for me!

Beyond the Coral Edge

Where the waves crash like a clumsy dancer,
The fish are plotting a wild romancer.
A crab in shades, looking quite slick,
Seems ready for a photo shoot, oh what a trick!

In clear blue depths, the mermaids giggle,
As dolphins crack jokes and wiggle.
A sea turtle drags its slow parade,
While seaweed whispers, 'Join the fun brigade!'

With snorkels on, we laugh and dive,
Bubbles rise, making us feel alive.
But watch your step on the slippery rocks,
Unless you fancy a dance with the flocks!

As sunset turns the sky to pink,
The fish all gather, it's time to think.
With laughter echoing through the shores,
I vow to return, who needs chores?

Garden of Evening Tranquility

In the garden where the gnomes abide,
They gossip softly, with grins tried.
Nearby a cat, with a sassy strut,
Claims this patch; it's her favorite hut.

Flowers chuckle when the wind does blow,
Leaving bees dizzy, in quite a low show.
A dandelion says, 'Look at me dance!'
While a stubborn weed demands a chance!

The moon peeks through, a cheeky glow,
While night jasmine spreads a fragrant show.
With squirrels chattering their late-night tales,
Even the crickets sing with their scales.

So here's to evenings that twinkle and buzz,
With nature's laughter stirring just because.
For in this garden of whimsy and cheer,
The world's a funny place, that's crystal clear!

Celestial Dance of Light and Shadows

Under the sun where shadows play,
The trees do tango in their own way.
A flickering butterfly, quick and spry,
Says, 'Catch me if you can!' before it flies high.

Clouds drift by like fluffy sheep,
Whispering secrets, then drift to sleep.
The sun grins wide, giving a nod,
While raindrops tickle the ground, oh what a prod!

At twilight's gate, the stars align,
While fireflies twirl like they own the line.
An owl hoots, 'What a fun affair!'
As raccoons prepare for a late-night square!

With laughter spilling from every nook,
The universe winks, like a storybook.
So join the dance, let your worries unwind,
In this cosmic giggle, peace you will find!

Secluded Shores of Serenity

On a beach where seagulls strut,
I tripped and fell right in a rut.
The sun shone bright, the sand was fine,
I met a crab, he said, 'You're mine!'

With flip-flops lost, I dashed away,
A little fish joined in my play.
We built a castle, quite sublime,
Until the tide came, perfect crime!

Palm trees swayed with every laugh,
I tried to dance, but did the half.
A shady spot to sip and dream,
While sipping coconut ice cream.

The laughter echoed, waves a-cheer,
As beach balls bounced, we had no fear.
Under the sun, all woes forgotten,
Life here is sweet, not too rotten!

A Symphony of Silence and Waves

The ocean hummed a goofy tune,
As I stumbled like a marooned baboon.
The waves waved back with foamy grace,
I nearly slipped—what a funny face!

Under the sun, my worries flew,
But then a crab nibbled my shoe.
I shooed him off, but he took the bait,
Is this beach a snack bar? What fate!

Shells played drums, the breeze chimed in,
I danced a jig, a goofy spin.
The sand, oh man, it made me sneeze,
While laughter echoed on the breeze.

With sunburned noses, bright and red,
I chased a pelican instead!
He snickered loud, he had his fun,
Who knew this beach could be such a pun!

Gentle Breezes and Glowing Horizons

The sunset winked, a cheeky tease,
I ran to catch it with the breeze.
But tripped on sandals as I flew,
And fell face-first—what else is new?

My drink umbrella turned to sail,
As seagulls gathered, telling tales.
With ocean's giggles all around,
My beachside antics know no bound!

A jellyfish whispered, 'Stay away!'
I laughed and danced, 'Not today!'
With waves applauding every move,
I feel the rhythm—gotta groove!

As night fell down, stars twinkled bright,
My friends and I had quite a sight.
With laughter bubbling, quite a scene,
Life's a beach, and I'm the queen!

Embrace of the Ocean's Caress

Embraced by waves, a silly sight,
A dolphin swam and stole my bite!
I called him Flipper, he gave a grin,
Splashing back, oh what a win!

As sunbeams danced upon my nose,
I waved at boats while striking poses.
But here came trouble, beach balls galore,
I dove for cover—what a score!

The tide brought messages from the deep,
'Find your lost sandals in a heap!'
The ocean giggled, like an old friend,
Saying, 'Don't worry, this is pretend!'

With laughter spilling, joy on show,
Life's a beach, and I'm the star of the show!
Under the sun, no need to fret,
This sunny circus, my best bet!

Celestial Shores: A Retreat

On sandy carpets, we all lie,
Building castles, oh so high.
But when the tide wants to play,
Down they tumble, oh what a day!

Seagulls laugh as they snag a fry,
Wingly acrobats soaring by.
With ice cream cones, we take a stand,
Melting quickly in our hand!

Palm trees whisper with cheeky glee,
"Dance with us, come set it free!"
Limbo low, or just take a stroll,
Swaying hips, spilling cola on the shoal!

Nighttime comes, lanterns a-glow,
Crickets hum as the stars put on a show.
Every chuckle carried on the breeze,
With sandy toes and hearts that please!

Where Time Slows Down

Under a sun that likes to tease,
We lounge around with perfect ease.
Sipping drinks that might just spill,
Lizards staring, with time to kill!

Flip-flops flop as we march away,
To find the snacks we clearly 'may'.
But then we trip, oh what a scene,
Rolling like we're in a routine!

Clouds drift slowly in a race,
Cheeky crabs scuttle with grace.
Each giggle echoes, it's all quite grand,
Except for the sunburn on my hand!

As the sun dips, the colors swirl,
Fireflies dance, we start to twirl.
Laughter bubbles, like waves at play,
Options for dinner? Maybe just 'Dorito' buffet!

Kisses of the Warm Waves

Incoming waves with friendly swoosh,
Crash on the shore, a jellyfish whoosh.
Salted kisses, a cheeky mess,
Who knew giggles could cause such stress?

Surfers riding a foamy crest,
Wipeouts happen, but they're the best!
Splashy laughter fills up the air,
Who's got sunscreen? Let's all beware!

Children splash, their laughter loud,
Building giggly dreams, oh, how proud!
Paddling fun with goofy grins,
Friendships made, let the sea begin!

As moonlight kisses the ocean's face,
We moonwalk back, with goofy grace.
A toast to the waves, the joy they bring,
Let's dance, let's sing, and take to wing!

Serenity Beneath the Treetops

Under canopies, we laugh and play,
Squirrels yell, "Hey! Don't take my hay!"
Swinging low, we dodge the leaves,
Nature giggles, it never deceives!

Hammocks swaying, a gentle sway,
Watching ants march on their way.
Breezes tickle, a playful tease,
Even the vines seem to giggle and squeeze!

Picnic spreads filled to the brim,
"Last donut!" echoes, voices whim.
Under the shade, excuse the clatter,
As crumbs tumble, oh, who cares? No matter!

Stars peek through when the sun bows down,
Laughing together, we wear a crown.
Serenade the night with stories stout,
And dream of adventures, never in doubt!

Where the Sea Meets Solitude

Sandy toes and sunburned nose,
The seagulls scream, while the tide just flows.
Coconut dreams and pineapple hats,
Beware of crabs that steal your snacks!

Flip-flops flying, oh what a sight,
Dancing with waves, "Surfing's alright!"
A beach ball bounces, a dog takes flight,
And sunbathers laugh from morning to night.

Sunsets paint the skies in gold,
But sunscreen jokes, they never get old.
A lounge chair here, a drink in hand,
Who knew sun lounging could be so grand?

But hold your pose, don't take a dive,
The lifeguard shouts, "You can't revive!"
With laughter ringing, we surf the air,
In our happy place, without a care.

A Mosaic of Blissful Moments

Bright colors splash where fun is found,
Each laugh a wave, all around.
Mango sips and popcorn fights,
We're primates mixed with beach delights!

A game of catch, why not with fish?
With splashes loud, we fulfill our wish.
The waves cheer in their frothy glee,
As crabs tango between you and me.

Umbrellas tipped by a playful breeze,
Naps cut short by the buzzing bees.
Cannonball splashes, a grand success,
While sandcastles rise to impress!

As beach towels ripple, friendship swells,
We create our world and cast our spells.
Every moment a treasure in play,
Life's beachside jokes brighten our day.

Whispers of Paradise Found

Beneath the palms, a giggle hides,
As ants march by, we run for rides.
Chasing waves with silly faces,
In sandcastle lands, we find our places.

A single flip-flop wanders off,
While I'm stuck here trying to scoff.
A picnic feast, with mismatched socks,
As laughter dances while time ticks and rocks.

Ocean whispers plot mischief right,
As jellybeans twinkle in sunlight.
Sunscreen battles beneath the sun,
Each goopy smear, pure laughter's fun!

The tide rolls in, the tide rolls out,
Wave after wave, we twist and shout.
We're tangled up in laughter's crown,
In our found paradise, never a frown.

The Embrace of Nature's Bounty

In gardens lush, the fruits extend,
But who knew vines would become your friend?
Banana slips and mango slips,
Nature's pranks, they make us flip!

The turtles gawk, quite judgmental,
While frogs sing loud, oh ornamental!
A pineapple hat? Why, oh why?
Fashion's lost in our fruit pie high.

Peeking through leaves, we giggle loud,
Chasing shadows, forgotten, proud.
The flowers sway to a tune we hum,
While bees of course play the drum!

With nature's bounty, we create our game,
From silly poses, there's no shame.
Together we dance, this laughter spun,
In nature's embrace, we're forever young!

The Silent Dance of Morning Dew

Morning dew drops start to roll,
Like tiny dancers on a stroll.
They twirl around with glee and cheer,
Hoping to tickle your sleepy ear.

With a light giggle, they greet the sun,
Jumping on leaves, oh what fun!
They sneak up close, then dash away,
Creating mischief at the break of day.

In the grass, they bounce and prance,
Making the flowers join their dance.
But watch your step, they might just flee,
Leaving your toes a little wet, you see!

So sip your coffee, take a seat,
While dew drops shuffle on tiny feet.
They'll spin and laugh 'til daylight's done,
These merry sprites, oh what fun!

Harboring Peace in Nested Sands.

In a sandy nook where seagulls land,
I found a treasure, or maybe just sand.
It giggles and whispers, 'Come play with me!'
But it's just a crab, as sassy as can be.

The sun takes a break under a palm,
While I search for conch shells, so quaint and calm.
But every shell I pick up and hold,
Turns to be a small rock, not treasures of gold.

The waves keep calling, 'Let's dance on the shore!'
But I trip on my flip-flops, oh what a chore!
With laughter and splashes, my worries all flee,
As I face off a wave that aims to soak me!

So here I sit, with grains in my hand,
Hoping for magic in this sun-kissed land.
With giggles and crabs, what could go wrong?
Even the sea knows where I belong!

Paradise Whisperings

In a hammock hung low, I hear the trees,
They gossip and giggle with the buzzing bees.
'Watch out for monkeys, they steal your snack!'
But I stay cozy with my sunhat on back!

The ocean waves waltz with the soft breeze,
Tickling my toes with playful ease.
I close my eyes, hear the locals chat,
About the great coconut who's rather quite fat.

The rainbow fish jump, making quite the scene,
As they flaunt their colors, so bright and clean.
I wave to a clam, who looks quite bemused,
As a curious gull drops down, slightly confused.

So here in this bliss, I lounge with delight,
With whispers of paradise fading in light.
Every silly moment a treasure to keep,
As laughter flows softly, like dreams in my sleep!

The Calm Beyond the Palms

Beneath the palms, a party's begun,
With coconuts dancing, oh what fun!
The sun's a jester, flipping a ray,
As I sip my drink, oh what a day!

The parrot's a singer, off-key yet bold,
Telling silly stories that never get old.
I join in the chorus, with laughter so bright,
As sandcastles wave goodbye to the night.

With mischief in the air, clouds drift around,
Making shapes of dolphins that nose dive to ground.
But watch for the shadows, they might just play,
Tagging the tourists who wandered astray!

So let's toast to this slice of blissful fun,
With laughter and frolic under the sun.
Every wave holds a story, every breeze a tune,
As I rejoice in this silly afternoon!

Elixirs of Island Stillness

In the shade of a palm, I take a nap,
A coconut falls, what a silly slap!
Seagulls squawk songs, quite out of key,
A serenade, performed just for me.

Lemonade laughter splashes in the air,
As I dance with a crab, do I dare?
The fish in the sea giggle as they swim,
Inviting me to join on a whim.

Tiki torches flicker with comical grace,
While I trip on my flip-flops, lose my place,
The island vibes tickle like a soft breeze,
Making my worries dissolve like cheese.

Life's a hoot under sun-bright skies,
Where even the waves wear mischievous ties,
So grab your shades, let the good times roll,
In a paradise where we lose control.

An Odyssey of Ocean Emotions

Oh, the ocean's a stage for laughter and glee,
With mermaids who sing off-key so free,
A dolphin dashes, playing hide and seek,
While jellyfish jive, oh so uniquely chic.

A crab in a tux, what a sight to behold,
Telling dad jokes that never get old,
As seaweed fluffs up like a wild green wig,
While I giggle at the octopus doing a jig.

Each wave that crashes has a story to tell,
Of clumsy sailors and fish that fell,
An adventure awaits in the salty spray,
Where every splash brings humor our way.

From sunsets that wink to sunrises that tease,
The ocean's emotions will surely please,
So let's set sail on this laughter ride,
An odyssey of fun with the tide as our guide.

Revelry of the Reggae Breeze

Feel the rhythm of the sun-kissed air,
With reggae beats that flatten despair,
A pineapple wears shades, lounging laid back,
While coconuts giggle, no need to unpack.

The palm trees sway like they've lost their mind,
Dancing to tunes, oh so unrefined,
Turtles on surfboards, oh what a sight,
With shades and surf wax, pure delight!

Every sunset's a party, no need to rush,
With drinks that sparkle in a coconut hush,
The hammock sways, a comical breeze,
Turning my nap into a fun-sneeze.

Basking in colors, I stumble and trip,
On sand that's as soft as a gentle grip,
In this joyful revelry, laughter is crowned,
Where the vibes are infectious, and joy knows no bound.

Sunkissed Calm and Melancholy

Here lies humor in the sun's bright glare,
With flip-flops howling, as I lose my pair,
The hammock groans, giving a silly squeak,
While my drink does a dance, so unique!

Seashells speak secrets of love gone wrong,
As starfish strut, singing their own song,
Each wave whispers sighs, mixed with a grin,
Telling me where laughter begins.

Coconuts tumble, serving smiles in rounds,
As crabs share gossip in comedic sounds,
The sunset paints skies with hues of surprise,
While giggles erupt like the evening tides.

Emotions collide in this blissful embrace,
With moments of calm and a funny face,
So let's toast to joy, and the laughs that we find,
In this oasis of bliss, where fun's intertwined.

Whispers of Palm Breezes

In the shade where coconuts grow,
Sandy toes wiggle to and fro.
Parrots gossip with a squawky cheer,
While squirrels steal snacks and disappear.

Lemonade in hand, I sip with glee,
A crab pinches toes—as bold as can be!
Seagulls dive, then swoop and swirl,
Claiming snacks in the beachy whirl.

Sunburns that only last a day,
'What sun?' I say while I sway.
A coconut falls with a startling thud,
I dodge to the side, avoiding the flood.

Every breeze carries laughter clear,
Mermaids giggle—though no one's here.
Underneath palm trees, life rolls by,
With a wink and a nudge, oh how we fly!

Serenity Beneath Sunlit Canopies

Sipping coconut from a spiky shell,
Every sip feels like a funny spell.
Crickets chirp, throwing a bash,
While I trip over my own flip-flop's clash.

The sun's a jester, with rays that tease,
Blowing kisses through the swaying trees.
A monkey's antics, a comedic sight,
As he pirouettes, oh what delight!

Sunbeams dance like they're in a race,
While I'm just grateful for a cool place.
Sticky ice cream drips on my knee,
An ant decides he wants it for free!

Laughing at shadows that play on the ground,
In this paradise, life's joys abound.
With silly hats and gleeful cheers,
We celebrate life without any fears!

The Lullaby of Gentle Waves

Waves crash softly, like tickling feet,
Under the sun, life's a joyful treat.
Seashells giggle, oh what a sound,
As I trip over the loose beach ground.

In a hammock, I sway with ease,
While the breeze whispers jokes through the trees.
A crab in a tuxedo waddles right past,
It's the beach's cutest comedy cast!

The sun sets in an orange glow,
With some dancing jellyfish putting on a show.
I laugh at the moon for being so round,
'Tis the funniest thing my life has found!

Each splash tells stories, tickling my soul,
A dolphin with sunglasses is the ultimate goal.
As night paints smiles across the bay,
We await tomorrow, with more fun to play!

Where the Mango Trees Stand Still

Mangoes hang low, a ripe buffet,
Evading me with a sneaky sway.
I throw my hat to get one free,
But end up splashing in the sea!

Beneath the trees, I find my cheer,
A parrot squawks, "Hey, over here!"
With every bite, the juice cascades,
Making me giggle as my shirt fades.

Grasshoppers hop with a jazzy beat,
Stepping in rhythm, they dance on my feet.
A lizard grins, plotting his way,
You'd think he's got a big dance today!

As the day rolls on, laughter abounds,
With silly shenanigans all around.
So here I rest, with no cares at all,
Awaiting more mischief with the mangoes to call!

Lighthouses of Dreamy Margins

In the haze, a lighthouse stands tall,
Seagulls squawk, they're having a ball.
A crab tries dancing, slips on a shell,
While fish debate which stories to tell.

With a wink, the beacon beams sharp and bright,
Bats wear sunglasses, what a funny sight!
A message in a bottle, it floats on by,
"Help, I'm lost! And oh my, the pie!"

Sandcastles crumbling, silly little feats,
As the tide giggles, with bubbly retreats.
Mermaids laughing, they join in the fray,
Trading seashells for fishy cabaret.

Coconuts rolling, they gather to dance,
Fruits compete sliming for some romance.
Cheers erupt, like waves from the shore,
In this whimsical world, who could want more?

Starlit Strolls on Foggy Nights

Under a blanket of winking stars,
We strut like penguins, dodging the jars.
Moonlight giggles, it tickles the trees,
While owls assume they're experts in ease.

Fog sneaks in, it's a slippery mess,
Trip over shadows, oh what a dress!
Fireflies dance with a boogie so fine,
Guiding our steps like a conga line.

Laughter echoes as we frolic in fun,
Counting the stars till we're almost done.
A raccoon wearing a hat joins our crew,
"Star-gazing's best when you've got a view!"

But watch out for puddles that sneak up behind,
They're cheaters, I swear, not being too kind.
Through whimsical chaos, we'll find our way,
With chuckles and jokes, we'll seize the day!

Ocean's Lullaby and Jungle's Kiss

Waves whisper secrets, a cozy refrain,
While trees join in, swaying without strain.
Fish in a chorus, they gurgle and croon,
"Join us, dear friends, we'll dance till the moon!"

A parrot cackles, mimicking a laugh,
As crabs form a band, they strum with a gaff.
Jellyfish juggle, with grace they will glide,
While turtles shimmy on the ocean's wide side.

Snakes slide with style, a disco delight,
Chasing their tails under soft starlight.
"Who's winning the race?" the turtles all say,
"Not me!" cries the snail, "I prefer the buffet."

So let's sway like the palms, feel the beat,
With silly sea friends, we can't be beat.
In this grand jest of life, we shall bask,
With giggles and joy, together we'll bask!

Luminescence in Softening Twilight

As daylight bleeds into twilight's embrace,
Glowworms debating their best hiding place.
A sloth with a dream, moves slow but is keen,
To catch every glow, sight unseen but serene.

Luminous blossoms open with glee,
Offering jokes to the honeybee.
Fireflies flutter, they tell tales so bold,
"Did you hear of the fish that turned into gold?"

As night tiptoes in, we wander with care,
Silly shadows leap, mimicking the air.
The minty fresh breeze wraps us in cheer,
While giggles erupt, scattering all fear.

In the dance of twilight, we twirl and we spin,
As the stars come out, let the fun now begin.
With laughter so bright, our spirits do soar,
In this glow of the night, who could ask for more?

Island Echoes in Whispering Tides

The beach is nice, but watch your toes,
As waves come crashing, oh how it goes!
Flip-flops flying, ducks in dismay,
"Aloha!" yelled Bob, losing his way.

Palm trees sway with a dance so grand,
But do they really know the moves, or planned?
Coconuts giggle, calling your name,
In this silly game, who's really to blame?

Sunshine spills onto the sandy floor,
A seagull swoops in, begging for more.
Cheese fries or chips? Decisions, oh dear!
Life's just a party, full of laughter and cheer.

With ukuleles strumming a tune so bright,
We sway and we laugh into the night.
Tiki bar mocktails with silly names,
Here on the beach, nothing feels the same.

Floating on a Sea of Surrender

On rubber rafts we bob and float,
But where's the prize? We forgot to note.
Mom's yelling, "Get down!" — we won't, not today,
As we splash in the sun, come what may!

Ice cream drips down, hot and sweet,
A seagull steals snacks — oh, what a feat!
With giggles and grins shared all around,
We find joy in the chaos that's truly profound.

Floating along, we claim the space,
But who's the captain? It's a messy race.
Sunscreen battles waged, slippery hands,
We're pirates of fun, with no maps or plans.

A rubber chicken floats by, what a sight,
"Is this the treasure?" we laugh with delight.
Life's like a wave, ride it till the end,
On this ocean of laughter, let's make amends.

Lush Haven Beyond the Horizon

Through green leaves rustle, a parrot squawks,
In the jungle, the monkey does weird walks.
Vines and branches twist with flair,
While we're tangled up without a care.

"Let's zipline!" screams Jim, what a notion,
As he flies by, flailing in motion.
Lemonade stands serve drinks that bubble,
In this lush haven, we stumble and tumble.

Mangoes tumble from trees above,
A feast that mocks the fruit we love.
With sticky hands and giggles so loud,
We're crowned the kings of this silly crowd.

As the sun dips down, the colors swirl,
We find a dance that makes our heads twirl.
On this lush escape, it's all fun and games,
In a place with no limits, and no one to blame.

Serenity in the Shade of Hibiscus

Under a flower that's big and pink,
We ponder the mysteries, sip and think.
But wait! There's a bee that's buzzing near,
"Oh no!" we shout, while sipping our beer.

Chairs in a circle, adults act like teens,
Playing cards while sipping on beans.
Sandy feet up, lounging with style,
A rooster struts by, taking a trial.

Lemon pie fights are the highlight of days,
As laughter erupts in these goofy arrays.
A hammock swings low, it gently sways,
With dreams of vacation in silly ways.

As night descends, the fireflies glow,
In the shade of hibiscus, laughter will flow.
A serenade of chuckles fills the night air,
Our joyful hearts dance without a care.

Shores That Hold My Secrets

On sandy shores, I lost my shoe,
With crabs making off, who knew?
The sun beats down, my hat's a kite,
I chase it down, what a silly sight!

Seashells whisper tales so grand,
Of froggy leaps and seaweed band.
I thought I saw a starfish dance,
Turns out it just gave my toes a chance!

The waves arrive with a teasing splash,
While gulls snag fries in an all-out clash.
I made a friend, a fish named Fred,
But he swam off, left me for bread!

As sunsets blush like overripe fruit,
I burp out laughter, a beachy hoot.
In this silly place, sunburned and free,
What will tomorrow's mischief be?

One Thousand Island Dreams

One thousand islands, all in a row,
Each one's a secret, I can't let go.
A hammock swings like a giant's chair,
I jump right in—who needs to care?

Coconut drinks were all the rage,
But the way I spilled? Just like a stage!
Palm trees whisper with gossip galore,
I promise to return, but they just snore.

An iguana winked, said, "Join my club!"
I tried to dance, fell into a grub.
With each gaffe, I make new friends,
Even if the laughter never ends.

The sun sets low with a fiery grin,
I wave goodbye to my silly kin.
In dreams tonight, I'll sail the seas,
With gumdrop clouds and chocolate trees!

Pathways Through the Peaceful Grove

In peaceful groves where giggles hide,
   I trip on roots, oh, what a ride!
The breeze plays tricks on my silly hair,
   Like it's auditioning for a circus fair!

Butterflies flirt, they dance and twirl,
As I try to catch them, I stumble and whirl.
A squirrel throws acorns like tiny rocks,
   I laugh so hard, I hear my socks!

Mushrooms wave hats, all dressed in style,
   They throw a party, stay for a while.
A raccoon named Rick plays hide and seek,
But he's too busy munching on crunchy cheek!

As moonlight joins this forest frolic,
   I trip again, and it's just iconic.
   In nature's lap, I feel alive,
With every blunder, I thrive and thrive!

Sun-Kissed Thoughts of Emptiness

Thoughts wander like surfboards at sea,
With empty coconuts laughing at me.
The sunbeams tickle, what a tease,
I chase my dreams as they flee with the breeze!

Flip-flops flapping, I'm in a race,
With shadows and laughter all over the place.
A seagull squawks, "Hey, what's your deal?"
I reply, "Just chilling, how about a meal?"

My hat flies off, a rebellious flare,
I shout, "Bring it back, you lazy air!"
The distant horizon waves "hello,"
While I trip on sand, putting on a show.

With every wave, a chuckle awaits,
In this silly world, I embrace the fates.
Sun-kissed, giggling, I roam the shore,
Emptiness dances—who could want more?

Gentle Currents, Gentle Hearts

In the warm waters, where fish wear hats,
The crabs dance waltz, while seagulls chat.
A turtle glides past with a cheeky grin,
Saying, "Take a break, let the fun begin!"

Under the sun, the beach ball flies,
While toddlers chase waves with wide-open eyes.
Flip-flops squeak in a slippery race,
A sandcastle king, claims his sandy space.

With piña coladas, small umbrellas in sight,
The sunburned tourists look quite a fright.
But laughter erupts, like bubbles in drink,
Here every worry just starts to shrink.

As sunset descends, they lift up their glass,
Toast to the moments that time needs to pass.
In this playful realm, where the sun never parts,
We find laughter and joy in gentle hearts.

Sun-Kissed Shores of Repose

On sun-kissed sands, kids bury their dads,
While laughter erupts, driving all of us mad.
Surfboards bobbing in a comedic way,
As they wipe out all hopes of a sporty display.

Beach towels spread, like colorful flags,
Sunscreen applied, a mess in our bags.
But a seagull swoops down for a feathery dive,
Stealing a sandwich and teaching us to strive.

Uncle Joe struts in his vintage swimwear,
Only to slip and send drinks everywhere.
With grins and a giggle, it's all in good fun,
As ice cream drips down, we know we have won.

As waves roll in, and the sky starts to blush,
We all gather round with a celebratory hush.
In this joyful spot, like sunshine's sweet dose,
We dance to the rhythm of sun-kissed repose.

Rapture in the Garden of the Gods

In the garden of giggles, where fruits wear a smile,
Bananas go dancing, it's quite the wild style.
The pineapples chuckle, the oranges sing,
As nectarines plot an uprising of bling.

Nearby, there's a parrot, with jokes up his sleeve,
'Why did the mango not quit? He believes!'
With laughter erupting amidst emerald hue,
Even the flowers find humor in dew.

Coconuts chuckle, under palms' gentle sway,
While the breeze shares stories of another day.
In this garden delight, peace makes a stand,
Where the ridiculous rules and joy is unplanned.

At dusk when the colors swirl, hearts take flight,
We share in the rapture, it all feels so right.
In the garden of cheer, amid laughter and logs,
We'll always chase joy, in this land of the gods.

The Luster of Evening's Embrace

Under the twilight, where colors ignite,
Fireflies flicker, like stars in the night.
The picnic's a party, with sandwiches stacked,
And ants join the fun, their snacks well attacked.

As the sun takes a bow, crickets start to sing,
We chuckle as someone makes a bee-keeping thing.
With laughter so loud, it tips into the breeze,
"Be careful, my friends, don't scare off the cheese!"

Laughter bubbles up from the shores of our dreams,
As marshmallows toast in whimsical gleams.
Even the moon, with its giggly sheen,
Winks at the chaos of this nighttime scene.

In the evening's embrace, all worries take flight,
Wrapped in the warmth of this joyful delight.
With friends all around, happiness-laced breaks,
We find the luster our hearts always take.

A Haven Beneath the Canopy

Underneath the leafy green,
Monkeys chatter and squirrels preen.
A hammock sways, I take a seat,
While sipping juice, oh what a treat!

Coconuts rain from high above,
While seagulls squawk, they think they're tough.
An iguana slips on a vine,
He surely thinks he's looking fine!

In this nook the worries fade,
No crowded streets or deadlines made.
I'll trade my shoes for flip-flops now,
And exchange my frown for a sun-kissed brow!

A sloth comes by with a lazy grin,
Takes his time, oh where to begin?
We'll share a laugh, a sunny drink,
In this haven, life's at the brink!

Island Solace in the Sun

On this soft and sandy shore,
Crabs dance sideways, what a chore!
With shades so wide and drinks so tall,
I'll take a sip, then drop the ball!

Palms sway gently to a tune,
While I start to feel like a baboon.
The sunburn game is quite intense,
I'm losing it, it's just not dense!

Flip-flops flop, my toes in the sea,
Fish swim by, they laugh at me.
A beach ball flies, I duck and dive,
In this bliss, I feel alive!

As evening falls with skies so pink,
I see a shrimp, it winks, I think.
I raise my glass with wild delight,
Island fun, oh what a sight!

Driftwood and Destiny

A piece of wood tells tales of old,
While I sip rum and feel quite bold.
Waves whisper secrets with a smile,
As seashells ponder life's long mile.

The tide is high, I'm feeling chatty,
A parrot squawks, oh isn't that ratty?
A crab joins in with sideways flair,
In this driftwood life, we're quite the pair!

Laughter rings where the seagulls flock,
As I build castles with my socks.
The tide comes in, my work's destroyed,
The beach is where chaos is enjoyed!

Driftwood dreams beneath the sky,
As I watch palm trees wave goodbye.
With every sip and every joke,
This driftwood life makes my heart stoke!

The Stillness of Sapphire Waters

In sapphire waves, the fish parade,
While I float by in a giant shade.
A dolphin flips, he takes the scene,
And I just hope my tan's still keen!

With every splash, my heart takes flight,
Trying to dodge a feisty bite.
A sea turtle grins with lazy grace,
While I'm just trying to keep my place!

The stillness here is pure delight,
Yet somehow I've lost my sight.
In search of snacks, I take a dive,
To find a treat, oh joy, I thrive!

As sunset paints the sea so bright,
I bid adieu to the fading light.
In sapphire waters, laughter rises,
For every moment here, surprises!

Lullabies Under Starlit Skies

Beneath the stars so brightly sewn,
The crabs are dancing, who could've known?
A lizard hums a sleepy tune,
While frogs conspire to steal the moon.

Coconuts fall with a plop and a splash,
While parrots giggle, making a clash.
The waves are swaying, a gentle rhyme,
As I sip my drink, it's party time!

Palm trees sway like they're doing a jig,
Touched by the breeze, oh so big!
The night is young, let's bring on the fun,
With laughter echoing under the sun.

So here we are, booties in sand,
Singing our hearts out, oh isn't it grand?
With mischief and joy, we will embark,
Beneath the star-riddled, silly park!

Respite in Hibiscus Blooms

The flowers giggle with a vibrant hue,
As bees buzz around, a wristwatch crew.
With petals wide and faces so bright,
They say, 'Stop and smell this, don't fight!'

A butterfly flutters, it's perfect and bold,
While ants have a party, all in a hold.
They march in sync, like they're on parade,
To la-la land, where fun can't fade.

The sun blinks twice, giving flowers a wink,
As I grab a drink, and almost sink.
With juice on my nose and laughter in tow,
I wonder how high a bee can go!

So let's frolic in petals, both wild and sweet,
Where every small stumble has a cozy seat!
In this joyful patch, let our spirits bloom,
For life is a garden, and I'm in full plume!

Glimmers of Kinetic Calm

The ocean waves play a teasing game,
When the sun dips low, it's never the same.
Fish jump high like acrobats brave,
As the sea turtle calls, 'Come, misbehave!'

A sprinkle of laughter on the beachy shore,
Dancing with shadows, we can't help but roar.
The hammock beckons, it swings with grace,
While crabs try to find the slowest pace.

Seagulls laugh, dropping fries from above,
As squirrels dispute on the meaning of love.
The beach vibes and giggles, oh what a mix,
In a world where humor does plenty of tricks!

So let's gather our chuckles and dive into spree,
In this festival of joy, come ride with me!
For where fun is abundant, we stay so calm,
As waves cheer us on with their rhythmic psalm!

The Rhythm of Resting Tides

Drifting along with the tide's soft sway,
Shells sing songs in a magical play.
Each wave a whisper, a chuckle divine,
As starfish applaud, oh how they shine!

A crab tries to dance, but trips on a shell,
He flips and he flops, oh what a spell!
The sun winks down, sharing its light,
As sea cucumbers snicker at the sight.

The breeze shimmies through, carrying cheer,
While dolphins spin tales that we long to hear.
With sand underfoot and hearts full of fun,
We ride the rhythm till the day is done.

So let's lay back and enjoy this glide,
Where laughter is currency, and joy our guide.
In this land of blunders, love spills and spills,
Together we dance, forever it thrills!

Sunset Serenade of the Islands

The sun dips low, a mango glow,
And crickets chirp a serenade,
A coconut falls with a silly thud,
As I laugh at it, quite unafraid.

The ocean winks, a gleam so bright,
The waves do a dance that's quite absurd,
A cocktail spills, oh what a sight!
My towel's a table for a grazing bird.

Palm trees sway with a comic flair,
Like dancers lost in a goofy trance,
I shake my hips, with zero care,
And join the breeze in a silly dance.

As stars pop out, like dots of cream,
I chuckle and giggle, my heart is light,
In this bizarre island floating dream,
Where laughter echoes into the night.

Cocoon of Coral Dreams

In a soft cocoon of reef and rays,
I find my thoughts drift like a boat,
An octopus winks, in a playful haze,
And gives me fashion tips—who would've wrote?

With fish in hues that steal the show,
They shimmy and shake in coral caves,
I clap my hands, go with the flow,
As bubbles rise—who knows, it saves!

A starfish grins, an artist's muse,
His five-point plan is quite bizarre,
He juggles shells, I just can't snooze,
In this underwater comedy bazaar.

As the ocean jeers with a giggling tide,
I waddle along on the sandy floor,
In this silly world, I just can't hide,
With all the chuckles and mermaid lore.

Swaying Palms and Gentle Hues

Beneath the palms that sway with glee,
I sip my drink, a splash of fun,
A parrot squawks, 'Look, it's me!'
As I splash my toes, the day is won.

The sky a canvas of giggly tones,
A watercolor of laughter spills,
While crabs in tuxedos roam like drones,
Chasing each other over the hills.

A breeze whispers jokes, so light and breezy,
It tickles me like a plump balloon,
The hammock sways, feels all too cheesy,
I bounce a bit—what a funny tune!

As dusk draws near, I chuckle still,
With stars that wink, a sight so grand,
In this lighthearted, jolly thrill,
Where joy is scattered across the sand.

Echoes of the Ocean Breeze

The waves come in with a cheeky laugh,
They tickle my toes, what a tease!
A floating duck, my laughter's staff,
As it quacks along with the playful breeze.

Seashells giggle as they tell their tales,
Of ships and fish and silly gnomes,
With every wave, the laughter sails,
Floating home to the ocean's roams.

A crab in shades struts down the shore,
With a swagger that would steal the scene,
I root for him, yelling, "Give me more!"
While seabirds swoop, the beach was green.

As night falls soft, the moon gives a wink,
The tide plays tricks, oh what a sight,
I take a step and, with a clink,
Join all the laughs in the quiet night.

Driftwood Dreams Along the Shore

A piece of wood with stories told,
It floats on waves, a sight so bold.
I sit and ponder what it's seen,
Was it a boat, or just a bean?

I gave it a name, Fred was it,
Together we'd fish, it was quite a hit.
But Fred just drifts, no rod to fight,
While I eat snacks from morning to night.

We chat about fish, and seagulls too,
He claims he's watched a pelican stew.
But who's to judge a wood's true quest,
In sandy dreams, we're both quite a mess.

So here we sit, the waves a-hum,
Fred keeps me laughing, the ocean's drum.
Life's a tide that ebbs and flows,
With driftwood dreams, who truly knows?

Castaway Reflections at Dusk

On a beach with no plans and sand in my shoes,
I spot a crab with some lacking hues.
"Hey little guy, where's your crew?"
He just rustles and scuttles, blue to view.

I build a palace not fit for a queen,
Out of shells and seaweed, my throne is unseen.
A wave knocks it down; I start from square one,
My kingdom of sand is forfeit, not fun.

I wave to the sunset, it winks, what a tease,
I call for the crabs, "Come on, join me, please!"
But they all roll their eyes, too busy with snacks,
Probably discussing their glorious tracks.

With a belly full of laughter and grains in my hair,
This castaway gig isn't entirely fair.
But as the stars gather, hearts won't rush,
I let out a chuckle, my spirit a hush.

Enchanted Isles of Soft Embrace

On a tiny isle where the breeze plays sweet,
I found a parrot who fancied a treat.
"Polly wants crackers!" he squawks out loud,
I laugh as I see him, a feathery cloud.

With coconuts rolling like sweet little balls,
I tumble, I laugh, as one gently falls.
The birds are amused, they've got their front row,
As I roll like a tumbleweed, fast and slow.

I'm king of this isle, the ruler of fun,
With sun and confetti, my day's just begun.
The lizards play tag, oh what a sight,
While I chase my hat that took off in flight.

But with smiles around me and laughter so grand,
I gather my treasures, keep them close at hand.
An enchanted place where the whimsy's ablaze,
In soft embraces, I'll bask all my days.

Beneath the Coconut Canopy

Beneath the trees where the coconuts fall,
I dodge and I weave, they're a risky sprawl.
A comical game of 'dodge the round fruit,'
I giggle and squeal, "What's next, a hoot?"

A monkey swings by, all grace and delight,
He throws down a nut, and it gives me a fright.
"Is this for me, or just your silly laugh?"
I take a deep breath, and then start to chaff.

The shadows play tricks, the breeze carries tunes,
As I dance with the breeze, twirling like balloons.
With each silly step, I'm a sight to behold,
The coconuts chuckle, their stories are bold.

So here in the shade, I sway with glee,
Life's a pirouette; I'm a coconut spree.
With laughs in the air and fruit up above,
Beneath this green canopy, I find all my love.

Valleys of Verdant Serenity

In fields where iguanas wear capes,
And grasshoppers dance in funny shapes.
A sloth just laughed, what a sight to see,
Chasing the breeze like it's the key.

Coconuts giggle, they can't be serious,
While parrots squawk, their tone so curious.
The palm trees sway, then stop for a chat,
Demanding punchlines like a comedian's hat.

A hammock swings, sways like a boat,
With every giggle, it begins to float.
And ants on parade march with great pride,
Wearing sombreros, they try to hide.

Clouds gather 'round for a tea party game,
And every raindrop has a silly name.
In valleys where laughter fills every space,
Fun for all ages, what a happy place!

Floating on a Cloud of Bliss

On clouds so fluffy, where dreams take flight,
Flamingos practice their ballet at night.
A narwhal plays a tuba, oh what a show,
While a cat in a hat steals the whole glow.

Rainbows burst with giggles, colors collide,
Balloons hold secrets no one can decide.
Unicorns munch on cotton candy clouds,
Surrounded by laughter, they form silly crowds.

Lemonade rivers flow, mix with the sun,
And sugar cane canes play a tune just for fun.
A surfboard made of chocolate, doesn't it gleam?
Let's float on sweet waters, not just a dream.

So jump up high, on marshmallow hills,
Dancing with dreamers and ice cream spills.
With laughter like waves that roll with great bliss,
We float down this dream where nothing's amiss.

Beneath the Celestial Canopy

Stars wearing pajamas wink with delight,
While owls in tuxedos take off in flight.
The moon flips pancakes, oh such a feast,\nWhile
squirrels recite poems, to say the least.

Beneath a canopy where night sings along,
The crickets form bands, performing their song.
Fireflies twinkle like disco balls bright,
Each glow brings a chuckle in the soft night light.

Bats wearing glasses get books from the shelf,
While raccoons sit reading, to learn 'bout themselves.
A comet zooms by, just to steal the scene,
Chasing after shadows, it's quite the routine.

With giggles echoing through shimmering skies,
Clouds whisper secrets, oh how they surprise.
In this silly haven, it's always a show,
Beneath the night's laughter, where dreams freely flow.

The Heart of a Secluded Haven

In a nook where the breeze shares rumors of fun,
A turtle in shades claims he's fast on the run.
While rabbits debate who hops the best,
A lily pad party says, 'Join us, you jest!'

The creek tickles toes as fish wear small hats,
While frogs leap to DJ, mixing tracks for the chats.
Fireflies light up the dance floor so bright,
And raccoons serve snacks, a midnight delight.

Lost in a book made of leaves and laughter,
A parrot rehearses for his big chapter.
Turtles gossip over cups of sweet tea,
In the heart of the haven, where wild's truly free.

With whispers of joy lounging in the sun,
And critters crafting tales that can't be outrun.
This secluded retreat is a vibrant bazaar,
Where laughter and friendship shine like a star.

Coral Reefs and the Call of Stillness

On coral couches, fish do lay,
While turtles snooze the day away.
The seaweed dances, waving cheer,
I hope the shark don't swim too near!

Crabs salsa on the sandy floor,
While clams just snore and snore and snore.
A starfish flips its lazy fin,
It's tropic life; let the fun begin!

Jellyfish float like puffy dreams,
In silly hats, or so it seems.
With echoes of waves that tickle the ears,
Nature's humor often appears!

Bubbles rise in gleeful streams,
Underwater giggles burst at the seams.
The ocean's call in vibrant hue,
Join in the merry, it's calling you!

Moments Cradled by the Ocean's Breath

Waves crash softly, tickling toes,
While seagulls squawk in funny clothes.
Sunbathers flip, like burgers grilled,
With sunscreen on, it's all been spilled!

Beach ball bounces, caught mid-air,
A kid trips over, no one cares.
Sandcastles wobbly start to lean,
A throne for crabs, quite fit for a queen!

Palm trees sway like they lost a bet,
While surfers chase waves like a pet.
The ocean whispers tales of fun,
Where every day feels like a run!

Sandy snacks much sweeter here,
Although some ants might disappear.
Laughter echoes, that's the plan,
Under the sun, all beach fans can!

The Hidden Paradise of Evening Stars

As dusk arrives, the fireflies dance,
While crickets chirp, a funny chance.
The stars come out in goofy glow,
Like disco balls put on a show!

Laughter fills the island breeze,
With jokes from trees that sway with ease.
A coconut drinks the sunset warm,
While beachgoers snicker at the charm.

The moon, a glowing slice of cheese,
Brings giggles from odd palm trees.
Waves chuckle, kissing the shore,
Nature plays, forever more!

With a sky canvas bold and bright,
The night wraps up in sheer delight.
Each twinkling star a wink and grin,
A cosmic joke, let the fun begin!

A Symphony of Nature's Stillness

The breeze hums low, a gentle tune,
While crickets join beneath the moon.
Laughter swirls in the silent night,
Nature's joke takes wing in flight!

With frogs in chorus, oh so loud,
They croak their songs to please the crowd.
The rustling leaves dance all around,
In nature's band, the joy is found!

Waves play maracas on the shore,
As seagulls add their cheeky roar.
The stars twinkle like they know,
The fun that lies below and grow!

In the stillness, humor sits,
Amongst the waves, the laughter flits.
Every rustle, chirp, and call,
Tells a story — a giggle for all!

Journey to the Pearl of Peace

In a hammock strung up to my knees,
A seagull lands, stealing my cheese.
Sipping coconut with a silly grin,
I'm on a quest where boredom can't win.

Fish flip and flounder, like they're on stage,
Making a splash, oh such a rage!
Sunshine laughs in a playful way,
As I try to tan my toes, come what may.

Barefoot on sand, what a wild plot,
Chasing crabs, they run like hotshots.
Each wave brings giggles, oh what a sight,
I might just build a sand fort tonight!

With gulls as my buddies, I'm feeling spry,
Tripping over shells, oh me oh my!
Paradise found, no passport needed,
In the laughing tide, my worries exited.

Mosaic Sea of Softest Hues

A sea of colors, like jelly beans,
Waves tumble soft in sunlit dreams.
Wearing flip-flops, I dance on the shore,
Tripping on laughter, who could ask for more?

Pineapples wearing shades, what a sight,
Dancing with coconuts under the light.
Seashells gossip, like best friends do,
Sharing secrets of the ocean's hue.

Wall-to-wall blooms, like nature's fun,
Quirky rocks tell tales of everyone.
A splash from the waves gives me a shout,
Nature's own party, there's never a doubt!

With each silly wave, I lift my toes,
Sprinkling happiness wherever it goes.
Collecting the smiles that wash on the beach,
In this colorful dream, joy's within reach.

Hidden Havens, Gentle Sighs

In secret nooks where palm trees sway,
I find my giggle in each ray.
A lizard winks, oh what a tease,
While I sip Punch with a hint of cheese.

Sunset whispers as the day runs low,
Coconut critters putting on a show.
Turtles in sunglasses, look quite absurd,
Chasing sunbeams, not caring, oh how stirred!

Breezes tickle while I nap away,
Waking to sunshine, what else to say?
Even the mangoes seem to smile bright,
In this cushy haven, everything feels right.

While I throw sand, making a grand mess,
The ocean just laughs, what a sweet jest!
With each gentle sigh and playful wave,
I claim this corner, perpetually brave.

Soundtrack of Sunset Reflections

The sun dips low, like a ball of jam,
While crabs do the cha-cha, oh what a slam.
Pineapple records spin tunes on the breeze,
Even the clouds seem to groove with ease.

Palm trees sway, like they're in a dance,
As the stars peek out, they look askance.
The ocean's chorus hums a sweet tune,
While I wave at the moon, like a chubby cartoon.

With flip-flops flapping, I glide on the sand,
Every grain's a note from this island band.
Dancing with shadows, I skip and I whirl,
In this dizzy moment, I give it a twirl.

As the last rays fade, I wrap up the show,
Whispering secrets only we know.
With laughter and light, we bid the day bye,
In the soundtrack of sunsets, I'm destined to fly.

Still Waters and Whispering Winds

Beneath the sun, we wiggle and sway,
The fish are laughing, they have their say.
Seagulls gossip, what a noisy crew,
While crabs dance sideways in the bright blue.

The sand tickles toes, it's quite absurd,
As I search for shells, I trip on a bird.
Palm leaves chat softly, gossiping too,
Oh, what a beach day! Let's start anew.

A cool breeze whispers, 'What are we missing?'
Soft drinks in hand, the sun is just kissing.
We've lost count of where our towels have gone,
But in this paradise, we just carry on.

So here's to laughter, and snacks piled high,
To sandy adventures, just watch your pie!
With each silly tumble and dip in the tide,
In nature's embrace, we cannot hide.

Matins of the Marine Mirage

The morning light casts gold on the waves,
While dolphins are plotting their funny escapades.
A clam with a grin offers up his best advice,
'Life is a chance, so let's roll the dice!'

The crab in the sand wears a top hat and shoes,
He clinks his filled shell with a drink made of juice.
Seashells are the currency—trade yours for a laugh,
In this comic utopia, we'll dance and cav.

Tide pools are giggling, frolicking with glee,
While starfish debate who's the best at a spree.
The seaweed is wavy, it's a dance floor so wide,
Shaking our finned tails, we're free for a ride!

We'll toast the waves with our cups full of cheer,
The humor of seashells rings loud and clear.
With every sunbeam painting our blissful day,
We laugh with the ocean, come join the play!

Serene Shimmers of the Sea

The sun beams down, a spotlight divine,
While turtles are spinning and sipping on brine.
Crabs in sunglasses, they strut and they pose,
'Who needs a carpet?' one clam boldly shows.

Waves crash like laughter, it's a joyous sound,
Jellyfish jiggle, oh what a round!
Octopuses offer a high-five or two,
With eight flailing arms, it's a crazy crew.

Laughter floats up with the puff of a breeze,
Starfish are snickering, it's sure to please.
On this sunlit stage, together we play,
Each splash tells a joke, each ripple a sway.

A conch shell declares, 'Gather around!'
Friends from the ocean, now join the sound.
In this shimmering paradise, fun never ends,
Just follow the giggles where the shoreline bends!

Capturing the Calm Currents

Whispers of breezes tease our tall hats,
While otters are practicing acrobatic spats.
The sun makes faces, it tickles the sea,
As fish make a fuss—'Look at me, look at me!'

Coconuts tumble, a competitive feat,
While flamingos do yoga—can you take that heat?
A porpoise breaks out the confetti just right,
Saying, 'Let's party! Come on, it's a sight!'

Mermaids trade stories, their laughter a song,
While dolphins take selfies, the zoomies go strong.
The tide pools are filled with giggles and splashes,
As rays of sunshine turn splashes to flashes.

So grab your sunscreen and let's fill our day,
With silly adventures in every array.
In the hum of the water, let's cherish our fun,
Peace found in laughter, we're never quite done!

www.ingramcontent.com/pod-product-compliance
Lightning Source LLC
Chambersburg PA
CBHW072218070526
44585CB00015B/1398